The Tao of Gardening

**A Collection of Inspirations Adapted
from Lao Tzu's Tao Te Ching**

Pamela Metz

Humanics Trade Group
Atlanta, GA USA

HUMANICS

The

Tao

of Gardening

Table of Contents

Acknowledgments

This book emerged from many relationships with other writers and their works, with students and colleagues, with friends and family. I wish to thank some individuals who have made this and previous works possible: Charlene, Ren, Cinda, Carol, Judy, Susan, Neysa, John, Kathy, Kate, Anita, Gin, Diane, Gruffie, Patti, Rick, Barbara, Kay, Lee, and Jan. Each person, in a special way, has contributed to the creation of The Tao of Gardening.

I am indebted also to the translators of Lao Tzu's classic work. They have made the timeless ideas available in the English language. Specifically, I have relied upon the works of Stephen Mitchell, Brian Walker, John C.H. Wu, and Gia-Fu Feng and Jane English.

Gary Wilson and Christopher Walker at Humanics Publishing Group have been supportive in the completion of this book.

Lastly, Lao Tzu, thank you for making a "way" for your thoughts to evolve, adapt and endure.

x

Introduction

Most books on gardening are read for information. Those books provide important details on the details of growing things. This book, *The Tao of Gardening*, is to be read for inspiration. Using English translations of the classic *Tao Te Ching* by the Chinese sage, Lao Tzu, the author has adapted the words and concepts to the universal human activities of gardening. In keeping with the spirit and form of the *Tao Te Ching*, there is some repetition of themes and ideas such as connections, balance, nature, interrelationships, letting go, harmony, and acceptance.

Feminine and masculine pronouns have been alternated throughout the chapters to acknowledge both genders and their engagement in gardening. The term "master gardener" is used to describe the accomplished or developed person who gardens. This should not be confused with the widely recognized term "Master Gardener" which is a designated term for people who have completed a proscribed course of study and who serve as volunteers in a wide range of community gardening services and activities.

This book can be read for pleasure, inspiration, and meditation. It could serve as a text for experiences of horticultural therapy, both formal and informal. It may serve as a healing balm for the gardener who seeks the spiritual path through the physical and intellectual processes of gardening.

Rod MacIver, in *Heron Dance*, writes

"The Tao Te Ching is a poem, a book, set of guideposts, leading to a way of being that is simple, that is harmonious. It celebrates the workings of nature and of the universe, the cycles of life, the cycles of water. Taoism grew out of pre-dynastic China, a time when people lived close to the land. It is a philosophy more than a religion - rather than attempting to define the Great Mystery, it espouses humble acceptance, gentleness and non-interference. The Tao is about a harmony that can be more often sensed than described or understood."

The Tao of Gardening, then, is a way of gardening that is a journey and a way of living. It recognizes the inner and outer spiritual dimensions of the many parts that make up the whole of gardening.

The Tao of Gardening

1. The Tao of Gardening

The way of gardening
is not what it appears to be.

Yes, it is working with the soil.
Yes, it is the beginning of all things.

Yet, it is full of mystery.

It is more than producing flowers and vegetables,
working with weeds and rocks, trees and grass.

Yet, these all come from the same source.
The earth gives birth to all these things.

In this darkness of soil,
In this lightness of sky
is a way to understand
the Tao of gardening.

2. Paradox and Weeds

Weeds may be seen as beautiful
and flowers may not be attractive.
Some people see growing things as desirable
while others may see growing the same things as
undesirable..

Good and bad are necessary parts of the whole.
In a garden, all are part of life.
Weeds become flowers,
flowers were once weeds.

The master gardener, therefore,
works with all things.
She learns to do nothing
when nothing is to be done.

It may be her garden,
but she understands
that it is larger than herself.

3. Pruning

If you overvalue some plants,
the plant will become overpowering.
If you become possessive,
you may lose your possessions.

The master gardener understands
that growing things
must be pruned.
Loss by pruning creates
growth and gain.
Pruning a third yearly
over three years
refreshes a plant.

The empty places become
full and healthy.
Taking away
is giving new life.

4. Never-ending

The Tao of gardening
is never exhausted.
It is being used by many,
but is never used up.

The possibilities are never-ending:
cultivating, planting, nurturing,
thinning, pruning, harvesting,
resting.

This cycle of life
has been here forever.
It is as old as the earth.

5. Seasons

The master gardener doesn't choose
from good and bad.
The gardener recognizes the
balance of all seasons.

Gardening in the Tao
is like understanding compost.
It is made of organic material
which has served one purpose
in one season
only to become something else
for another purpose
in another season.

Each thing has its own seasons.
Stay in harmony with
the seasons of your garden
and you may find balance
in your life.

6. Mother Earth

Mother Earth is like the Tao:
filled with empty space
yet full of life.
Many worlds are created
on her shoulders.

We are always grounded in her.
She is always present to us.
She offers us infinite possibilities.

Gardeners understand
that we are held
in the comfort of her arms.

7. Life Cycles

The cycles of life
have always been so.
Why is this?
Because the life cycle
provides for others,
it has no needs for itself.
It is present for
all living things.

The master gardener waits
so that growth may begin.
He plants the seeds
but does not make them grow.
He prunes the trees
but does not create the fruit.
He seeks the life
but can not prevent the death.

Fulfillment comes by understanding
the cycles of life.

8. The Importance of Water

Water nourishes all living things.
The master gardener understands this.

Like the Tao, water gives life
to all plants,
weeds as well as flowers.

In gardening as in life,
follow these ways:
in planting, select a variety of seeds;
in watering, be generous;
in weeding, be mindful;
in pruning, be light-handed;
in cultivating, be careful;
in harvesting, be grateful.

By being graceful in your garden,
by not competing or comparing,
you embody the importance
of water and the great gift
it is to life.

9. Excess

When you water too much,
there may be flooding.
When you over -sharpen your tools,
they may lose their edge.
When you work too hard,
your muscles will protest.
When you fertilize too much,
you may kill the plants.
When you depend on others' approval,
you may forget your own joy.

Do your work in the garden,
and then rest.
This is a way to peace.

10. Stewardship in the Garden

Can you remember why you garden
and practice caring for living things?
Can you keep your heart as open
as a tender bud?
Can you see the flowers even
though they grow in weeds?
Can you allow the seasons
to come and go?
Can you understand that the garden
takes care of you,
even as you take care
of the garden?

Sowing, nurturing and harvesting.
Giving, receiving, resting.
It is possible to have these things
without controlling them.
Being a steward in the garden
has its own rewards.

11. What Is, and What Isn't

Clay pots are empty,
yet it is the emptiness
that we fill with dirt.
They are porous to
allow the dirt to breathe.

Trellises create a framework,
yet the vines fill the spaces.

Hoses are hollow,
creating space for directing
the flow of water.

Land lies fallow,
waiting for new growth to begin.

We think of what is,
yet depend on what isn't.

12. Pallette

The garden is full of colors.
Our senses are overwhelmed:
tastes,
sounds,
textures,
life.

The gardener surveys the garden
and remembers the original plan.
She understands the ebb and flow
of seasons.
Staying open,
she enjoys it all.

13. Caregiver

What makes the best garden?
Can a garden be a failure?

If you worry about your garden
being good or bad,
you lose the world of possibilities.
Standing firmly in your garden,
you see the miracles unfolding.

Give yourself to your garden
and trust in the beauty of it all.
If you provide care for the garden,
you are a caregiver for a part of the world.

14. Connections

There is something of
the mysterious in gardening
that cannot be heard, seen or held.

Standing on the earth
we connect with worlds
beyond our imaginations.

Gardening has no beginning
and no ending.
It continues even though
the snow covers the earth.
We are part of the seasons
and continue the connections
throughout the year.

15. Early Gardeners

The gatherers who discovered
the power of seeds
created the possibilities
for us to settle in one place.

Families and communities were
formed around the gardens
of the ancient ones.

Patience was required
to trust the life in the dormant earth.
Do you cultivate this patience
in your own life?

The master gardener understands
that after sowing,
she waits to reap.
When the harvest comes,
she is grateful to those
who have come before.

16. In between

By being open in your garden
you may find peace.
Inspiration comes
in unexpected ways.

Each one of us
is part of the whole.
We mirror the cycles
of the universe.

Understanding the lifecycles
of all things,
open to the way of the Tao,
we are aware of
beginnings,
endings,
and everything in between.

17. Master Gardener

A master gardener does not force
the growth in his garden.
Sometimes we do not
even know he exists.

A gardener who forces the garden,
in his eagerness, may destroy it.

A gardener who works
and then steps back
allows the garden
to become itself.

18. Balance

When there is too little water,
the plants shrivel and die.
When there is too much water,
the seeds are washed away.
With too much sun
or too much shade
the plants cannot fulfill
their promise.

A master gardener
remembers these things
and works to create balance
in her garden.

19. Simplicity

Too many tools
can crowd the garden shed.
Too many plants
can prevent full growth.
Too much digging
can destroy growing things.

Simplicity in the garden
cultivates natural growth
and peace in the gardener.

20. Gardeners and Non-Gardeners

Gardeners are always thinking
about their gardens
even in the seasons
of cold and snow.

Non-gardeners are unaware
of gardens, even
in the seasons
of warm and light.

Gardeners buy magazines,
peruse seed catalogs,
foster seedlings
and dream of planting.

Non-gardeners
read for pleasure,
watch television,
go for walks,
and dream of other things.

Gardeners are different
from non-gardeners;
they make the earth
beautiful for gardeners
and non-gardeners alike.

21. Just Enough

Gardeners at one
with the Tao
create energy in their work.

How can this be so?
Being with the Tao
gives freedom to experience
new ways, new garden paths.

Because the gardener
does not grasp for the Tao,
She remains in the Tao.

Her garden then,
has just enough
of whatever is needed.

22. The Tao in the Gardener

The way is in each one of us.
Balance comes from being out of balance.

When the Tao is in the gardener,
the gardener is peaceful.
He is a model for others
by doing his work in the garden.
Because he is unaware,
others become aware of him.
Because he gardens for the process,
his garden flourishes.

By being himself, the gardener
enjoys the Tao in the garden
and the Tao in himself.

23. Preparation

The Tao of gardening takes preparation:
knowing yourself,
knowing the soil,
knowing the weather,
knowing the seeds,
knowing your dreams,
knowing when and how
to put them all together.

A gardener who is open
to all these things
is part of the Tao.

A gardener who does not prepare
may lose the possibilities
of the Tao of gardening.

When you are prepared,
when you are ready,
trust the processes of nature
and your garden will grow.

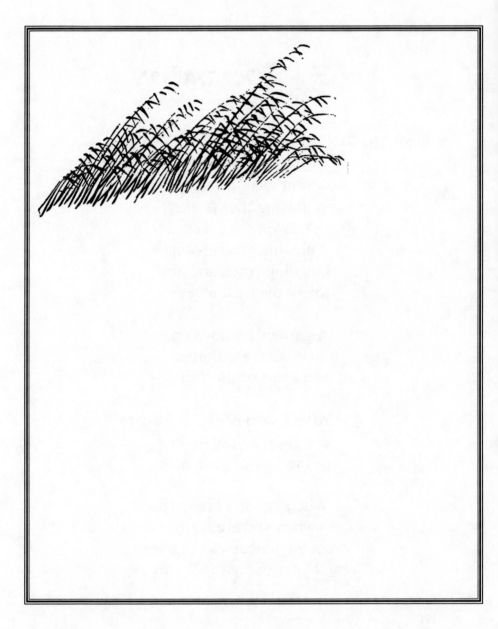

24. Grounding

Kneeling on the ground,
the gardener feels secure.
Going too fast,
planting too soon,
puts the plants at risk.
Looking only at the harvest
prevents the cultivation of all things.

To be grounded in your garden,
pay attention to each step.
Doing this,
letting go,
the harvest comes

25. Before Cultivation

Before cultivation, plants grew naturally.
Before gardening, everything
was left to chance.

When people discovered
how to plant seeds
and stay for the harvest,
the face of the earth was changed.

Civilizations begin with cultivation.

The Tao flows through
the history of gardening
making possible
all things.

26. At Home in the Garden

The garden is home for many things.
Being at home in the garden
is possible for those
who love the earth.

In the creation of patterns
and colors
and food,
the gardener
experiences the world
without leaving home.

If you are away
from your garden,
you may lose touch
with the cycles of growth.
You may forget
why you first began.
You may find,
upon return,
that no one is home.

27. The Good Gardener

A good gardener stays open
and knows she is never finished.
A good designer follows
her creative guides.
A good farmer stays free
of preconceptions
and experiments with possibilities.

The good gardener then
shares her knowledge
with others,
gives away plants and seeds,
composts materials for later,
and wastes nothing.

It is no secret
that wisely using all resources
is part of being
a good gardener.

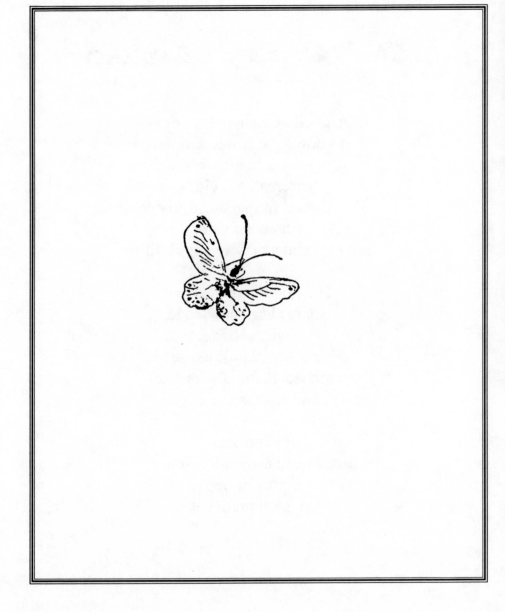

28. Pollination

Both female and male
are needed in gardening.
The Tao knows this
and is in the balance
of all things.

Choose for beauty and bounty,
staying aware of
bees and butterflies.
By keeping the balance,
you, too, are part
of the natural balance of things.

In gardening, see your
work as part of the world.
Bring order and life to your space.
Doing this, you embody
the spirit of Tao,
and co-create
harmony in living.

29. A Time for Everything

In your garden
you become aware
of the world.

The world is mysterious
and remains unknown.
Stay within the sacred circle
and appreciate the miracle of life.

In the garden, there is a time
for everything:

a time for work,
a time for rest;
a time for planting,
a time for harvest;
a time for water,
a time for sun;
a time for pruning,
a time for grafting;
a time for darkness,
a time for light;
a time for growing,
a time for dying.

The gardener knows all these things
and does not try to change these processes.
Although it feels like
there is never enough time,
the gardener knows
there is time enough
for everything.

30. Forces in Nature

Working with the Tao in the garden
means understanding the forces of nature.
Learning to pay attention
means watching the weather
and acting accordingly.

The gardener does his best
and then waits.
He knows that much
is beyond his control.
Trying to control the forces of nature
is not working with the Tao.
Because he understands this,
he does not try to influence others.
Because he has confidence in himself,
he remains free.
Because he works
with the forces in nature,
his garden is in harmony
with the Tao.

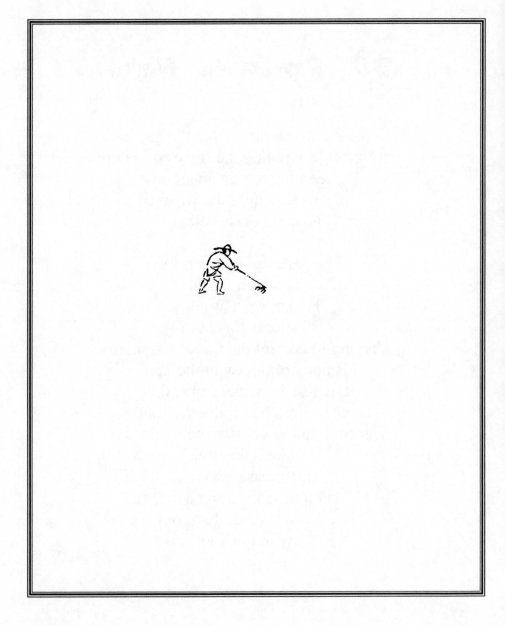

31. Gardening Tools

Gardening tools are necessary
for creating a garden.

The first tools are the gardener's
heart and hands,
vision and hope.
Together they create a place
for growing.

Shovel and trowel,
rake and hoe.
These tools make a home
for seeds and plants.

Watering hoses and sprinkler heads
direct the precious water
to continue growth.

Clippers and loppers,
saw and scythe
remove the old
to nurture the new.

Approaching the garden
with compassion and hope,
the gardener makes beauty
using all the necessary tools.

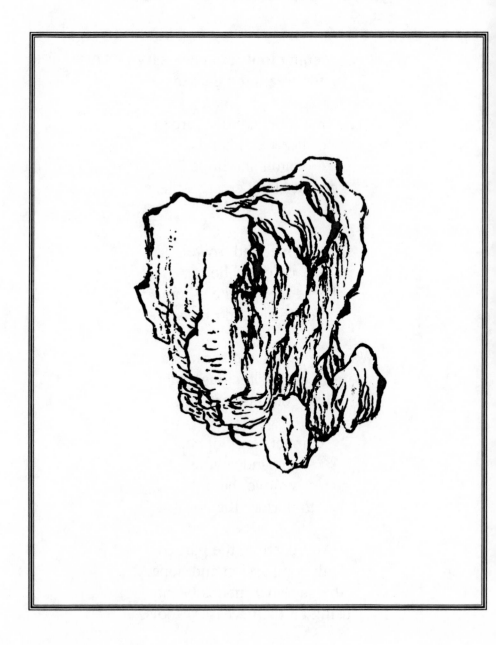

32. Unseen Energy

The Tao is unseen energy.
Small and large,
it remains a mystery.

If all people could see
our world as a garden,
we could foster
an environment of peace.

We could be gardeners
of the planet.

If our lives were balanced
with work and play,
if we knew when
to begin and when to stop,
we would be using
this unseen energy.

Each piece is part
of a larger whole.

33. Knowledge and Wealth

Knowing your garden is helpful;
knowing yourself is important also.
Working the soil is part of the path;
working yourself is a form of wealth.

Having the wisdom to know
how much is enough,
you have great wealth.
When you understand that everything ends,
your spirit remains free.

34. Miracles

The Tao is part
of the miracle of living things.
Everything is connected
to the Tao, yet these
connections cannot be seen.

Gardening reminds us
of this connection of all life.
We are dependent upon
the production of life
from the earth,
yet we forget to take care
of the earth.

The miracles endure
as long as we maintain
the balance of life
and remember our connections
to the earth.

35. Daily Tao

Daily Tao in the garden
prepares us for being in the world.
With grounding in the soil,
life becomes grounded in the Tao.

Because the Tao is invisible,
people wonder what it is.
Because it can't be heard,
people wonder about the silence.

Because it can not be used up,
it is always available.
Doing daily Tao
means being aware
of what is
and what isn't.

36. Harvest

Before you can prune something,
it must first be allowed to grow.
Before you can weed the garden,
the weeds must take life.
Before you can harvest something,
it must first be created.
This is how things are
in the garden.

Soft plants grow in hard soil.
Slow growing plants may
become larger than fast growing ones.
Working in the garden
reveals mysteries.
Nonetheless, the harvest comes.

37. Contentment

Tao in the garden does nothing,
but all things are done in the Tao.

Following the natural cycles
of light and dark,
sun and moon,
people experience
the simplicity of life.
When gardeners see this,
they can be centered in the Tao.
When this happens,
there is a feeling of contentment.

When people are content,
their hearts are full.

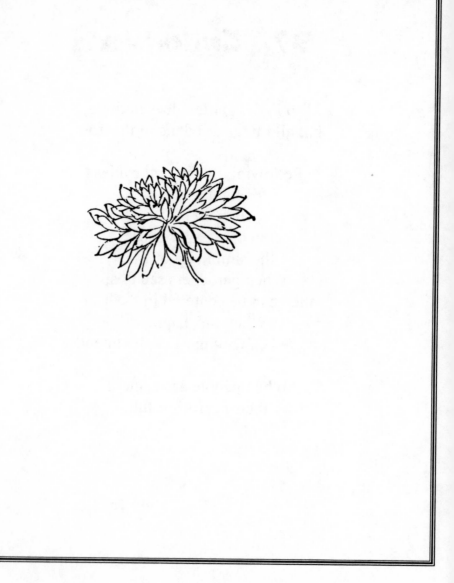

38. Power of Gardening

The master gardener realizes
the power in gardening.
Without effort,
she recognizes this truth.

Creating the conditions for growth
requires good judgment.
Making compost uses discarded materials.
There is a time to work the soil
and a time to let it be.

When gardening, be aware
of the whole and not just the parts.
Know the seeds as well as the plants.
By staying aware, the gardener reaps the harvest.

39. Meditation

When gardening in the Tao,
the gardener remains centered in the world.
There is peace in the garden.
Earth, sky, water and plants create
a place to meditate.

With too much interference
this harmony is disturbed:
plants die, the earth cracks,
and the garden loses its peace.

The gardener who knows these truths
understands the importance of process.
She practices a moving meditation.
As she shapes the garden,
she is also shaped,
becoming a part of the whole.

40. Doing/Not-Doing

Gardening requires doing
and not-doing.

The earth is the source.
From this comes all gardening.

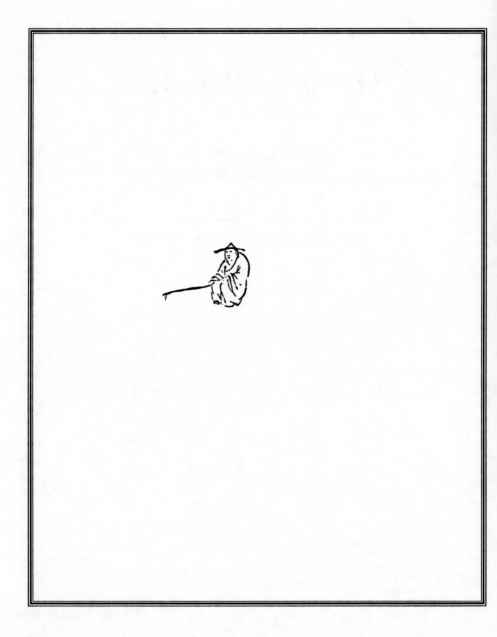

41. Humility

Gardening is done by
all kinds of people:
some are serious,
some are playful,
some remember,
some forget.

It is important to remember
there is paradox in our work.
Dormancy seems hopeless
Water makes floods and also droughts
Weeds are plants too
Sun and darkness nurture life.
from death comes life.
Insects help as well as hinder.
Too much growth can ruin the garden.
Too much effort may destroy our dreams.

The Tao of gardening is not visible.
Still, the gardener understands humility.

42. Reproduction

How do we understand
the way things are?
Beginning with one,
others are created.

Reproduction comes from
dividing plants,
saving seeds,
running roots.
Sharing plants,
passing them on,
is one of the
joys of gardening.

All things come from the Tao.
Propagation comes from the Tao.
Reproduction of living things
creates harmony in the garden
and creativity in the world.

43. Silence

In the garden
words give way to actions.
Work comes from doing.
Silence is full of sounds
of wind, birds, insects, plants.

The gardener at work
teaches without speaking.
This is the way of the Tao.

44. Happiness

What pleases you in the garden?
Sowing or reaping: which is best?
Planning or weeding: are they necessary?

When you care only about what others think,
it is difficult to know your own thoughts.
When your pleasure comes
only from your own harvest,
the process may not be repeated.

When your happiness comes from
seeing what you have
instead of what you do not have,
you are present for every possibility.

45. Planning

Plans come as visions:
all things are possible.
Perfection is seductive,
yet, is it really desirable?

When plans become reality,
new life is created.
Planning and reality are related,
but are not the same.

The gardener plans and then
understands the new life
that comes from planning.
She creates the beginnings
and then lets go,
shaping the garden
as it grows.

46. Taking Risks

Creating a garden
in the way of the Tao
means taking risks
along the way.

Don't be afraid of experimenting.
Plant a tender tree.
Select an exotic flower.
Try an unusual vegetable.
Facing the unknown
is a good lesson for life.

There is joy
in being unafraid
of failure.

47. Waiting

Working in your own garden
you are in touch with the world.
Working in the earth
connects you with all people.

You discover that
knowing is always incomplete;
understanding is elusive;
waiting takes time.

The gardener travels
through time and space,
weaving a web
with all other gardeners.

48. Mastery in the Garden

Seeking information,
knowledge is accumulated.
Reading books,
taking classes,
seeking others,
all contribute to knowing more.

In the Tao of gardening,
it is important to let go.
By letting go of some things,
what remains becomes clearer.

Mastery comes by understanding
that each thing goes its own way.
Too much interference
creates obstacles in the garden.

49. Caring for Everything

The gardener who cares for all things
is truly a master gardener.

He becomes a steward of the earth,
a shepherd for others,
and a creator of a healthy environment
for all things.

He nourishes trust in the connections
of all living things.
He is patient with those
who do not understand.

This kind of care-fullness
is not always understood.
The gardener understands this
and continues to care for all things.

50. Investment

When a gardener invests
in the gardening process,
she understands that
this is the way of all things.

Fully engaged, she knows
that she, too, is part
of the process
of life and death.

Knowing this, she is free
to engage her energies:
working and resting,
investing and reaping,
until the cycles are complete,
and ready to begin again.

Pamela Metz

51. Love of Nature

In the garden,
all things are part of the Tao.
A love of nature
guides the gardener in his work.

This love provides the basis
for every thing:
plants, seeds, cuttings and grafts.
All are nurtured, protected,
watered and fed.
Trusting nature
creates the garden.
Loving nature leads
to understanding the Tao.

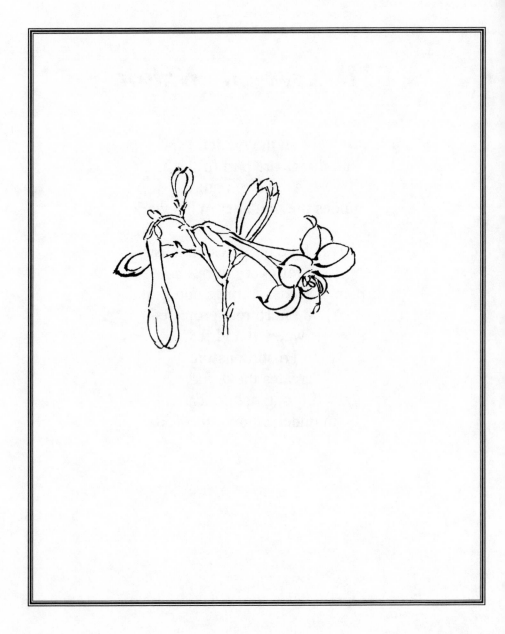

52. Heirloom Seeds

History precedes today.
Heirloom seeds have survived,
bringing the past
into the future.

The origins are not always clear.
When you taste the tomato,
you experience the source:
texture, taste, color, size.

The old gives birth to the new.
The new becomes the seed
for the future.

Treasure the heirlooms,
they transcend time.

53. No Gardens

Following the Tao
in gardening is clear,
yet people become lost.

Stay in balance with your garden
and you will know the Tao.

When balance is lost,
land is forgotten.
When gardens disappear
to buildings and parking lots,
when there are no gardens,
people lose sight of the Tao
and of themselves.

54. Inspirations

If you are inspired by the Tao,
your roots will run deep.
When you hold the Tao close,
your garden will flourish.

When the Tao is central
in the gardener,
she embodies trust
and faith and wisdom.

Her garden grows
and becomes an example
for others to see.
A harmonious garden
is possibility
for the entire planet.

Follow your inspirations
and your garden follows you.

55. Seedlings

When your garden is in the Tao,
you are as supple as a seedling.
It is fragile, yet holds
the promise of tomorrow.
It responds to the sun
and fills with the rain.
When it is nurtured, it becomes
a tree, a bush, a dream.

When the gardener
is receptive to these mysteries,
he is not disappointed.
With faith in the potential of seedlings,
he is in awe of the transformations.

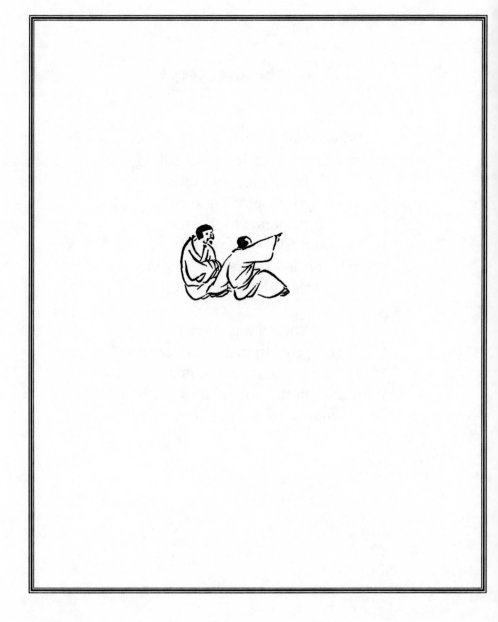

56. Patience

Some gardeners are without words.
They know but do not say.

Patience is required in the garden.
Too much or too little
can create problems.

The Tao is patient.
It does not force,
does not take,
is without desires.
It lasts because
it gives without limits.

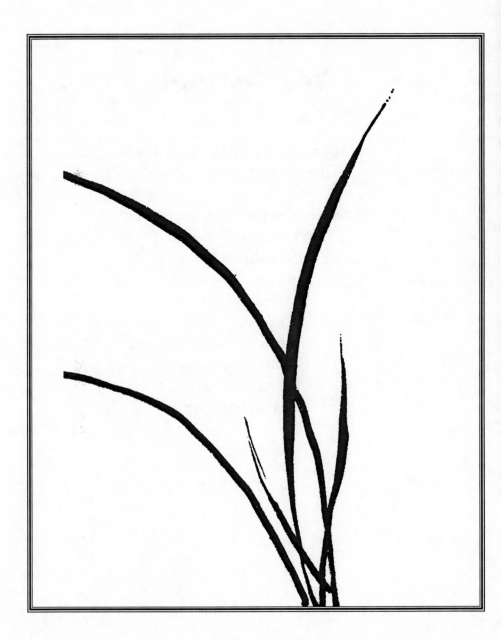

57. No Control

In the garden
you may learn about the Tao.
When there is too much control,
there may be resistance.
The harder you try,
the less control you have.
The more you relax,
the greater the rewards.

The master gardener knows this:
I trust the process
and the plants grow on their own.
I stop worrying about the weather
and the weather happens on its own.
I forget about my garden
and there is a surprise each day.

Remembering that much
is beyond my control,
I enjoy the unfolding
of the daily mysteries.

58. Setting an Example

When a garden is planted in peace
the neighborhood notices the change.
When a garden is neglected
this is noticed too.

The gardener may not be aware,
yet each part of the garden
sets an example for others.

Noticing the ways of the gardener,
others create peace in their own gardens.

59. Composting

Making good use of organic material,
the gardener nurtures the soil.

Understanding the process of birth
and death and birth again,
frees the gardener from regret.
She recycles the dead
to enhance new life.

Able to say goodbye
to this year's
blossoms, leaves and fruit,
she welcomes the next generation
in her own small composted garden.

60. Cultivation

Cultivating a garden is like
the loving guidance
of a small child.
Too much hoeing will ruin
the tender plants.

When your garden is centered
in the Tao,
you will cultivate it
and know when to stop.

Standing back, you can
appreciate what you have done
and what needs to be left undone.

61. The Life of a Gardener

When a gardener begins his work,
all energy flows toward it.
Plans, seeds, moisture, fertilizer,
are directed toward the garden.

In this centeredness, the gardener
takes on a life of creation:
mistakes are made,
teachers are consulted,
discoveries emerge.

A gardener's life becomes
part of the Tao:
relief is found
in working the soil.
Rewards come
in unexpected ways.
The sun caresses
his spirit.

62. The Center of the Garden

When you place yourself
at the center of your garden,
you are centered in the universe.

The value of the garden
is beyond money
and beyond time.
Like the Tao, no price
can be placed upon it.

When helping a new gardener
remember to teach her
about the Tao.
This is as valuable
as knowing about
soil, seeds, and sun.

Why is the Tao important?
Because the Tao
is the journey of gardening.
When lost, you find your way.
When mistaken, the garden forgives.
Stay at the center of your garden
to find the Tao.

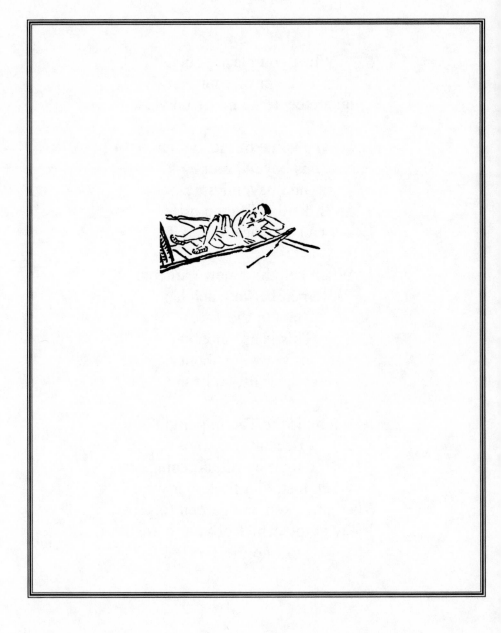

63. Difficulties

Doing without working,
thinking beyond borders.
When you see the whole,
the parts make sense.
If you work with difficulties
when they appear,
the whole garden benefits
from the efforts.

The gardener who does not try
to be great becomes great.

Finding small difficulties,
he attends to them.
He doesn't mind the inconvenience;
therefore, the difficulties disappear.

64. Making Changes

Seedlings are easy to nurture.
Loose soil is easy to cultivate.
Dry sticks snap at a touch.
Small seeds are easy to scatter.

The master gardener makes
changes as the need arises.
She knows that mighty forests
grow from small seedlings.
A new garden begins
with a single shovel of dirt.

By pushing things too fast
you may regret it later.
By picking fruit too soon
you miss the sweetness
of the mature fruit.

The master gardener understands change
by following the natural course of things.
Staying centered, she sees the beginning
and also the end.
Starting with nothing,
she does not worry about loss.
She has learned to let go.
She enjoys the process of gardening
and gives her heart to all living things.

65. Ordinary Gardens

The early gardeners
were aware of their blessings.
They shared their harvest
with each other.

When people are all-knowing,
they are hard to teach.
When they are looking for answers,
it is the time to show them a way.

If you want to be an expert,
remain open to the unknown.

An ordinary garden
is a thing of beauty.
Being satisfied with this garden,
you encourage others
to create their own
ordinary gardens.

66. Terraces

Water flows downhill
to create pools, ponds and lakes.
Building terraces slows
the water's flow.
There is power
in slowing down.

Gardening has power
by following the flow.
Guiding the water,
the gardener finds her home.

By understanding
the flow of water,
the gardener comes
to understand herself.

All water returns to the sea.
The sea sustains us
by its very presence.

67. What the Garden Teaches

There are those who may not understand
how gardening and the Tao are related.

Others may accept possibilities
but do not apply them in their gardening.

To those who are self-reflective,
these words convey some meaning.
For those who practice
the Tao of gardening,
these ideas grow like weeds.

The garden has these things to teach:
vision, perseverance, love of life.
Creating a vision, the gardener
realizes his dreams.
Persevering, he follows
the path of nature.
Loving life, he contributes
to life.
Open to the garden's teachings,
the gardener connects with the world
and with himself.

68. Working With Nature

The best gardener
respects the challenges of the garden.
She keeps the garden
always in her mind.
She follows the seasons
of her landscape.

The master gardener understands
how to work with nature.
She does not compete
with wind and hail and drought.
Nor does she compete
with other gardeners.
It is the spirit of gardening
that guides her in her work.

69. Yielding to Nature

Nature knows how to yield.
The soft gives way to the hard.
Water yields to every thing.

In gardening it is sometimes
better to wait and watch.
Sometimes it is better
to just let go.

This has been known as
letting nature take its course,
creating a garden in a natural way.

By understanding nature,
you understand yourself.
You are a part of nature
and a part of your garden.

When facing the forces
of nature, you survive
by yielding.

70. The Heart of the Gardener

Understanding the Tao
is not too difficult.
Practicing the Tao
is possible for most people.
Difficulties may
be present in the mind.

These teachings have been
available for a long time,
yet few have understood.

If you want to know the Tao,
look into the heart of a gardener.
When the Tao is present
there is harmony, patience,
balance, and wisdom.

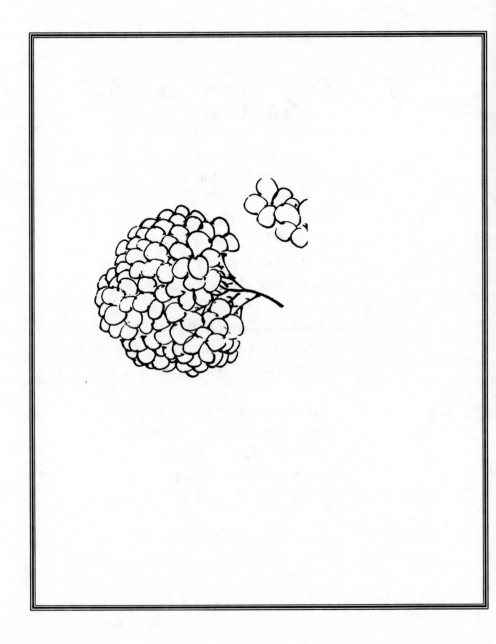

71. Healing and Growth

Can you admit
that you don't know?
When you think you know,
you stop asking questions.
Healing and growth
come from openness
to the unknown.

The master gardener
can live with not knowing;
therefore, he continues
to heal and grow.
Plants heal themselves
and continue to grow.
Growing plants can
heal a gardener's spirit.

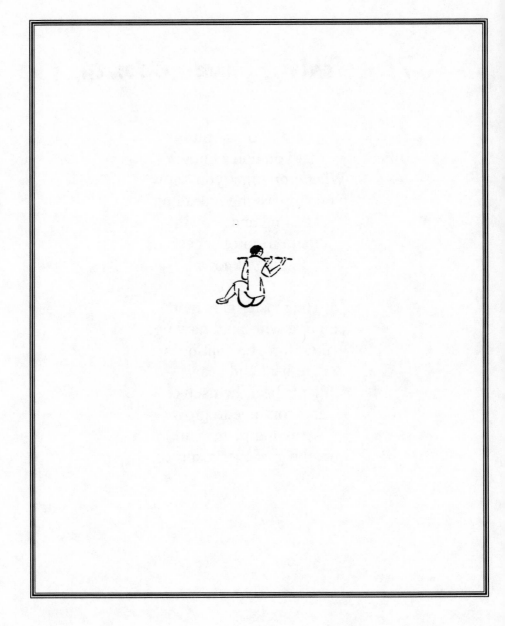

72. No Substitutes

There is no substitute
for the wonders of the garden.
Without this experience
people seek enjoyment indirectly
from sports, television, movies.

The gardener understands this
and serves as an example to others.
She teaches without words
and remains steadfast
in her garden.
She finds pleasure
in her work and it
becomes play.

She understands
that there are no substitutes
for her work in the garden.

73. Relaxation

The Tao of gardening
is relaxing and peaceful.
Without form and words,
without planning and effort,
it becomes itself yet again.

Your garden is part of the universe
and, though it is small,
like a hologram,
it captures the essence
of the whole.

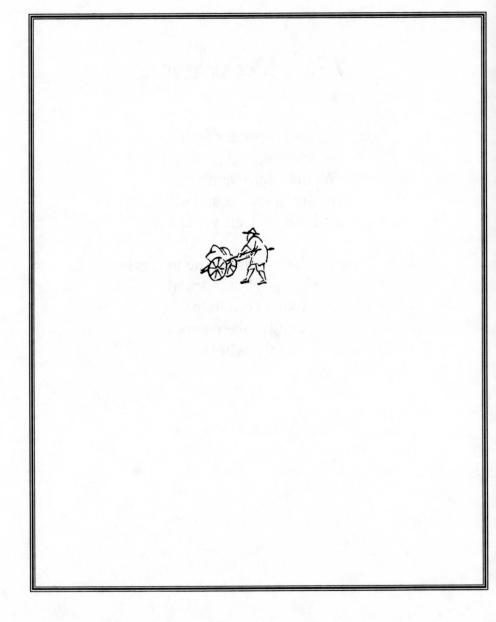

74. Change, Change, Change

The master gardener knows
that every thing changes.
He is ready to let go of all things.
Because he is unafraid of endings,
he is free to enjoy the beginnings.

He knows that the future is unknown.
He keeps his tools ready
and is open to many possibilities.

75. Spirit and Inspiration

The garden is available
for spirit and inspiration.
It provides food for the body
and for the soul.

Trust the process in the garden
and you will see the progress
in your own life.

76. Flexibility

Learning to be flexible
is a lesson in living.
Like new plants,
we are flexible and promising.
When we cease to grow,
we become brittle and uncompromising.

The rigid and firm
can be easily crushed.
The gentle and flexible
can survive.
Bending with the wind
prepares us for
the storms of tomorrow.

77. Generosity

In the garden, the Tao
is like a balancing scale.
When one side is too heavy,
the other requires more weight.
Keeping balance between
too much and too little,
the Tao seeks harmony in all things.

The gardeners who work
too hard
are not in balance
with the Tao.

The generous gardener
can continue to give
because her wealth is unlimited.
She is in harmony with her garden
and at peace in her world.
She reflects the generosity
of the soil, the sun
and the gentle rain.

78. Moisture

Forms of moisture
create energy in our world.
Water flows so that
we may grow.

Forms of softness and gentleness
eventually survive the rigid and hard.
Most gardeners realize this,
yet many cannot practice it.

The master gardener stays
centered even in the
middle of drought or flood.
He waits while nature
takes her course,
and proceeds after the storms.

Truth in gardening
takes many forms.

79. Learning from Mistakes

In the garden,
mistakes happen:
seeds are over watered,
shade plants are placed in the sun,
fertilizer is over applied,
watering is forgotten,
hollyhocks overshadow the sweet peas.

It is not helpful
to place blame.

The gardener
learns from her mistakes
and continues with her dreams.
She creates new visions
and lets go of the old.

80. Peace

When the gardener enjoys his work,
he is at peace.
He appreciates working
with his hands
and doesn't need diversions.
Because he loves being at home.
he doesn't need to go away.
There are many distractions,
yet they go unnoticed.
The gardener enjoys his home
and the pleasures of the garden.
In spite of the fact
that the world is enticing,
he enjoys the world
in his own small plot of land.

81. Tao in the Garden

This ending is really
a beginning.
True gardeners understand
this way.

The master gardener
embraces the Tao
and is able to include
all things.

The Tao nurtures by stepping back.
Thus, Tao in the garden
remains unbidden
and always there.

Bibliography

Bender, S. *Everyday Sacred.* San Francisco: HarperSanFrancisco, 1995.

Cleary, T. *The Spirit of Tao.* Boston, MA: Shambhala, 1993.

Dillard, A. *Pilgrim at Tinker Creek.* New York: Harper & Row, 1975.

Dillard, A. *Teaching a Stone to Talk.* New York: Harper & Row, 1982.

Feng, G., English, J. *Tao Te Ching.* New York: Random House, 1972.

Fields, R., Taylor, P., Weyler, R., and Ingrasci, R. *Chop Wood, Carry Water.* Los Angeles, CA: Jeremy Tarcher, Inc., 1984.

Findhorn Community. *The Findhorn Garden.* New York: Harper & Row, 1968.

Fleischman, P. *Seedfolks.* New York: HarperCollins Publishers, 1997.

Handelsman, J. *Growing Myself: A Spiritual Journey Through Gardening.* New York: Penguin Books, 1996.

Kincaid, J. *My Garden (Book):* New York: Farrar, Straus and Giroux, 1999.

Mah, A. Y. *Watching the Tree.* New York: Broadway Books, 2001.

Matott, J. *A Harvest of Reflections.* New York: Ballantine Books, 1998.

Metz, P. *The Creative Tao.* Atlanta, GA: Humanics Publishing Group, 1997.

Metz, P. *The Tao of Loss and Grief.* Atlanta, GA: Humanics Publishing Group, 2000.

Metzner, R. *Green Psychology.* Rochester, VT: Park Street Press, 1999.

Miller, R. *As Above So Below.* Los Angeles, CA: Jeremy P. Tarcher, Inc., 1992.

Mitchell, H. *Henry Mitchell on Gardening.* New York: Houghton Mifflin, 1999.

Mitchell, S. *Tao Te Ching.* New York: HarperPerennial, 1988.

Murray, E. *Cultivating Sacred Space: Gardening for the Soul.* San Francisco: Pomegranate, 1997.

Norris, K. *Dakota: A Spiritual Geography.* New York: Ticknor & Fields, 1993.

Sarton, M. *Journal of a Solitude.* New York: W. W. Norton & Company, 1973.

Walker, B. *Hua Hu Ching: The Unknown Teachings of Lao Tzu.* New York: HarperCollins, 1992.

Woodin, M. *The Painted Garden.* Philadelphia: Running Press, 2000.

Wu, J. *Tao Teh Ching.* Boston, MA: Shambhala, 1989.

About the Author

Pamela K. Metz lives in Denver, Colorado with her companion, dogs, cats, and gardens. She teaches at the University of Denver and is a recreational gardener.

Other Taoist Titles from Pamela Metz and Humanics

The Tao of Loss and Grief
ISBN 0-89334-335-8

The Creative Tao
ISBN 089334-255-6

The Tao of Women
(With Jacqueline Tobin)
ISBN 0-89334-237-8

The Tao of Learning
ISBN 0-89334-222-X

order online at:

www.humanicspub.com

CPSIA information can be obtained at www.ICGtesting.com
Printed in the USA
LVOW050846190712

290551LV00002B/20/A